I0471635

BIBLICAL BUSINESS BONES

11 WAYS TO Success

Easy Efforts & Simple Sense Strategies

By: Minister Lawander D. Harris
In The Light of His Word Ministry

Copyrights page

CONTENTS PAGE

Business quotes

© Yanny Natashah - Sometimes, the hardest decision made is the right thing to do.

© George F. Burns - Define your business goals clearly so that others can see them as you do.

©Vance Havne - The vision must be followed by the venture. It is not enough to stare up the steps - we must step up the stairs.

© Kahlil Gibran - Work is love made visible. And if you cannot work with love but only with distaste, it is better that you should leave your work and sit at the gate of the temple and take alms of those who work with joy.

© Colin Powell - Avoid having your ego so close to your position that when your position falls, your ego goes with it.

© Abigail Van Buren - If we could sell our experiences for what they cost us, we'd all be millionaires.

© Theodore Roosevelt - Whenever you are asked if you can do a job, tell 'em, 'Certainly, I can!' Then get busy and find out how to do it.

© Ralph Waldo Emerson - Practice is nine-tenths.

© Stephen R. Covey - if we keep doing what we're doing, we're going to keep getting what we're getting.

Recipe for Personal Success ...

Find a need that beats your drum

Create a plan, then make a dent

Trust that your reward will come

And credit them as heaven sent

(Unknown)

Introduction

IS YOUR LIFE SPINING OUT OF CONTROL? ARE YOU
TIRED OF FEELING LIKE YOU'RE NEVER GOING TO GET
THINGS ACCOMPLISHED? GET TO THAT GOAL? MEET
YOUR DESTINY? OR HAVE YOU TRIED TO DO
BUSINESS AS USUAL AND FAILED?   NO WORRIES…

The Father had a Method for your seemingly Madness.

The word <u>METHOD</u> means several things. Put the shoe that fits
on, and wear it to step out of your mad place into your happy-life
place. Here we go…

METHOD MEANINGS:

Method: Is a procedure, technique, or way of doing something,
especially in accordance with a definite plan:

Example: There are three possible methods of repairing this
motor.

Method: Is a manner or mode of procedure, especially an
orderly, logical, or systematic way of instruction, inquiry,
investigation, experiment, presentation, etc.:

Example: The empirical method of inquiry.

Method: Is an order or system in doing anything:

Example: To work with method.

Method: Is an orderly or systematic arrangement, sequence, or the like.

Now that you know what it means. My question to you is which manner will you make your dream happen? You must settle in your mind right now that you're going to establish a plan and accomplish it. No looking back – only moving forward.   How will you solve your problem or answer with a solution, the world that's waiting for what you've got? Will you be fashioned with the character to do something different? Will you dialogue with yourself the appropriate words of wisdom? Are you ready to position your life in a new way - with a new manner of walking? What's the best way for you to succeed for yourself and family?

SUCCESS METHOD #1 (Ways)

So what you're a female. Who says you can't be a business minded one? You are meant to be the best person you can be. Listen to me ladies. God has given you talents and gifts to use for your success in life. And when you become that strong-confident and financially fit woman God created you to be then you will really feel **FREE.** There is nothing that feels as good as being independently **FREE.**

Free to dream. **Free** to live. **Free** to run. **Free** to turn your talent into a business. **Free** to work on your own terms. **Free** to live life as you should and as you like. **Free** to start your church. **Free** to be founder of a particular foundation. And yes, even **Free** to travel. **Free** to do whatever it is that makes you happy, if it's meaningful and pleases God, and fits into his purpose for you. **Free** to feel enabled to help someone less fortunate. **Free** to feel good about your accomplishments. **Free** to see your life take on significance. **Free** to work for the Kingdom of God, while your money works for you. That's why the first success method we're going to talk about is called **WAYS.**

WAYS = With All Your Support

Weather your business is one of sole proprietorship, S Corporation or LLC, you will need support. Whether you're starting a mom and pop shop or doing a home based business you're going to find the word support keeps popping up. You want to always seek for support when you're starting any kind of venture. **For example:** If you're getting a new ministry off the ground, founding a foundation or non-profit organization. The key to success will always start with the type of support you have. The support you will glean and the support you will give. That's why the first business method I want to motivate you to pursue is a little word called <u>**WAYS**</u>.

'**WAYS**' is simply a business word I learned to use in my business and ministry pursuits. It stands for: <u>**"With All Your Support."**</u> Likely, common sense tells me no matter what I do in life I should always yearn for support from others. And nine times out of ten we will win when we do so. You can find help in many ways. There is no shortage of knowledge and information these days, seeing we live in the age of information.

Especially with the internet, research and the overwhelming resources we find online. But although we have these innovative digital technologies, which I'll talk about in more detail later on, we still have a need for the human touch. I bet you hate calling a business and getting those annoying answering cycles that just prompts you to push more numbers until you've gone through the whole numbers cycle. Only to be disconnected. It's a crackup.

That's exactly why I suggest you find ways to still communicate even though the technology makes it tempting to not do so. I'm not talking about being the same as those people who just push an autopilot button and that's it, or come in a shed a few tears for humanity and then go shopping. Well that's not it. We need people- connections and relationships to succeed in life. There will always be a need for another human being to help us. Speak with us. Coach us. Mentor and support us with our endeavors of life. We even need a person to straighten us out, or keep us straight.

Side Note: by the way, thanks for letting me help in whatever small way I can. As you'll find in pretty much most of my material, I write just like I speak. Most of the creative writings God have blessed me to share, come from my life he's given me to live and experience and make mistakes and get back up and do it again. So I enjoy writing self-help and inspirational materials. I realize my calling is to Motivate and elevate, to encourage and help those who can't for themselves. The name God gave me for ministry one day while in my prayer closet back in the 90's is called: 'In the light of his Word Ministry'

Biblical Business Bones is a book of business, life and ministry. But I'm not going to intimidate or manipulate you one way or the other. That's not why I'm here. But I am here specifically for the Lord's work and for your success. First off, i very strongly believe we can't be – if we can't see. And if one's in the dark then they need to move toward that light so they can see, right?

Anyway, my passion is to reach out to you in a good way. My goal with this book is to as well, help those who are less fortunate and who most likely are just coming into their faith walk with Christ and getting their feet wet with understanding about their...SELF-WORTH.

So don't think this is going to be hard, because it's not. This book is just another resource to help my fellow – SISTERS, and God's daughters who may want to better themselves by starting a business or encouraging ministry of sorts.

So, to the mother, housewife, domestic engineer, stay at home mom or independently challenged woman out there this is for you.

You can be whatever you want to be. You can do whatever your heart says you can. If you believe your own heart - do you believe it? Well the bible says as a man/ woman think in his/her heart so is he or she.

You may have never thought about doing a small business, working a job from home, or creating a service of some kind to enrich the lives of others. But guess what? That's exactly what you need to do. Now a day's things are not getting better. And because of the economic down turn and crisis everywhere things are only going to get worse. But Christ has given you and I keys to the kingdom to pull through these bad old times.

That's why I encourage you to please think about it seriously. What can you do to help yourself and family? What has God called you to? Whatever it is, don't worry he'll provide for it. Just get moving in the right direction.

This book is meant to be an easy effort encourager that will cause you to rise up to a better you with a better life. Are you ready?

Power Key: The Wise Woman Builds Her House. So that's what you and I were meant to do. Are you obeying God with this one? Right now as you handle your Biblical Business Bones Book, you will start on your track to success.

Look at life as a big old football field. Sometimes we get to play the game and make the touchdown. And here's the bonus, we get to even score sometimes. And on the other hand, we can't forget that this game of football is a team sport. That simply means we'll need each other while playing the game. So don't be afraid to join in. Someone's got your back just like you have theirs. That's why we all must yearn for support. You're the one responsible for seeking out that support. How do you do that? By getting connected with whomever it is that will help you. Coach you, egg you on, celebrate you and so forth.

Here are some examples:

- The boss on the job needs his employee just as much as the employee needs the boss.
- A mother needs the baby just as much as that baby needs its mom.
- Two spouses need each other just as equally.

No man's an island to himself. We need each other. God designed our destinies that way. Even God doesn't want to be alone. He's always pursuing you to come be with HIM. So whatever God starts, let's not try and do away with. Everything He originally formatted was good. And in your Business it's no different.

In business, career or ministry, God has already set up what we call 'the divine connection or a prominent hook-up. Those moments and people are usually right in our own backyard. See we're too busy many times standing in the front door. There we are, standing at a gaze in the front doorway, most likely picking daisies in our mind. While all along you're just letting in the flies. You know - Those pesky little critters that bug you to no ends.

Now I realize you're looking over your beautiful lawn that's been scorched by the sun. Or maybe you're dazing into the big open meadow. That field across the way. Wondering where your prize is. Wondering where your prosperity lies. Everything's quiet and the paths are clear you say. But there's just one problem. There's no movement from what we can see from this view. But don't panic. The secret is and has always been waiting for you right in your own back yard. You know the place many of us never think to look. Ah…the wonder of back yards!

It's the place where the dirt is hardly disturbed and similarly, the place where if we make an effort to just glance first, we may just surprise upon something good, satisfying and great. That's right my SISTER. Looking out the back door is no small thing. By doing that you may suddenly find a golden key which just may happen to be your idea, adventure, or resource to make your rich.

Just think about it.

The resource is right in front of your eyes, mind or just sparks up into your heart. Whew! So let's say you recognized your key. It was hidden in the dirt in the backyard. You barely saw the tip of it sticking up. You removed the dirt and saw it had some possibility of being more. So you took it in the house, polished it and used it. And found out it was the one that opened up your success. Isn't that awesome? All it took was a little bit of effort and responsibility.

Now remember, SUCCESS is when your life becomes more restful, easier and simpler. Whatever that is for you it will be very – very satisfying. Why is that so? In conclusion, it's because the key will include the fullness of not just money, but love, peace and humanity. (That's true success)!

I can speak so well about the backyard scenario because I had my own personal encounter with the backyard. Let me explain: I was tired of working in the corporate field for over 20 years so I quit my job and took my 401K and sunk it into a business. One that I was so sure I was still passionate about, but the business flopped. I went under and had to close down my "little Gourmet Shoppe."

So I figured, I'm out here now in the business sector and I need to keep trying things until I get something to work. You know it's true that a business minded person will try and try until they succeed. A true business person never gives up easily. They always come back for more. You know why? It's inside of them from the beginning of the foundation of the world to be a business person, to be free and independent some kind of way.

Well as my story goes. I tried one venture after another. But a lot of them were not what they promised to be or didn't do what they claimed to do. Just schemes to get more money from a sucker like me. But how many know that if we never plant a seed we'll never get any kind of harvest? I'm sure many of you knew that. Anyway, while I was doing all of my various business ventures one day I came to a screeching halt. I was frustrated and tired. I felt a little burn out as well. It seemed like everything I tried I was a day late getting to it and many of those things only appeased me. They did not truly satisfy me.

I had come to the end of my rope with all this business stuff. I had looked out over that big field in the front doorway and jumped into it with both feet running. But eventually, I got swallowed up by the over whelming business of technology and had to rest my brain from overload. I had to go somewhere and sit down and go within my inner self, so I could stop going without.

Without what you ask, without purpose and fulfillment.

This fulfillment of purpose was the seed inside of me that was dormant. I knew that because deep- deep within my bones I was supposed to do something with either a business or ministry in my life. And that would be the thing that would not only satisfy and gratify me. But that which would satisfy those attached to me. See? Then the Lord God revealed it to me. And after he did, I was able to use that resourceful key to open up many other doors. That was Gods purpose all along.

Now, weather you have no money, a little money or a lot of dough, these strategies work. They are everyday efforts we all must use in order to keep a mind set for staying on top of our game in life. There's no time for crying or giving up. You have no time to waste on throwing in the towel. Being a woman has only made you strong. And even if you've already launched your selfless efforts, being a woman who's done that, only has made you stronger.

It's true. I did that. Why, because even at that time I didn't understand the yearning inside me to be something different than what I saw myself as. You've heard the cliché that says 'if you want something different you must do something different'; well this is what was going on inside my belly.

Yes I said the word "belly." A seed is conceived. An idea is lying dormant. You at first don't pay it any attention. Then you realize it's getting bigger. You become restless and uncomfortable, till that seed starts to soak up all the water it can. This seed idea is the creative part of you. It needs to have space, just like a picture needs to be laid out on a canvas. Now do you get the picture?

You and I were created to be more than we are. When I say that, here's what I mean. If you're never more than just you – you'll never fulfill a greater purpose in life. Your purpose deals with a quad of "B"s:

better,

bigger

built up

being

So here's what that should look like: You as a person in life, business or ministry must become an even better individual with a bigger capacity to hold more. So that you can turn and build others up and this is the satisfaction of your being, as a human. There's nothing that feels as good as giving. That's why the cliché is so true. Try it sometimes and see what happens to you.

The concept is to place (you) in the way to HELP others, which brings us to our second method of success.

SUCCESS METHOD #2 (Help)
HELP = Here on Earth to Love People

I got a question for you. How are you going to help people if you are stuck in your own world or caught up in you all the time?

Let me tell you something. Never go out your door for being too embarrassed that you don't have enough to help anybody except you - your four - and no more. Instead, change your mind set. When you can see yourself growing to a point of where you're no longer afraid of taking a risk on trying something new, then you're on your way. And once you get on that path this is a big breakthrough!

You were meant to be a strong woman full of balance purpose, pose and passion. This means you've looked past the syndrome of "I'm all about myself". How many more designer purses can I collect, how many more celebrity shoes do I need to fill my closet with? You say, "But I'm the lady or woman who has never had the luxury of designer anything." You say… "I've never had a fancy hairdo, Pedi or manicure."

Well I'm sorry about that. I think every woman desires and deserves to have a nice manicure once in awhile. But weather you've had that privilege vastly or never had it at all, this book is still for you!

Let's take the woman who has lavished herself with extravagance. Even at the expense of taking the milk out of the child's mouth. If that's been so in your life, then you've gone about it the wrong way.

SELFISHNESS: is a mindset that must be done away with in order to see true success.

Let's look at the word and its meaning:

To be selfish is when someone has devoted all their time to caring only for themselves. They are concerned primarily with their own interests, benefits, welfare, etc., regardless of others.

And the Synonyms: mean the following:

Self-interested- self-seeking - egoistic; illiberal, stingy.

Wow, this is all negative. Now let me clarify that it's OK to go after your goals in life that are going to make you a better person to help someone. Remember: I said you'll always have to pull someone else up after you get yourself up. That's not being selfish. In fact, if you never better yourself for your children, family and others, then that's being selfish.

The selfish we're speaking about above is about when a person's always making sure they gratify their own fleshly-materialist desires. It's them first then, others last and God out of the picture all together. If this is happening, then you'll never get around to seeing about the others you left in the background.

Don't let vanity creep into your picture. If it does you'll regret it later. Vanity will cause you to become responsible for someone else's suffering. Remember I spoke about the mother who seeks after her own gratification at the cost of taking milk out of the baby's mouth. Well I have witnessed it. I've actually seen mothers just like this.

Their mind tells them that at the time their own needs or wants arise, the children can wait. (This is a selfish mindset) something everyone must get rid of if they find they don't have the right motive behind their serving.

View the following examples and make sure you're not found in any of these categories. If so, you've got some more work to do. God will not allow you to be blessed if you're bringing a curse upon your house and children with selfish motives.

EXAMPLES OF SELFISH ATTRIBUTES

The Low – to No Income persons

- A mother went out to party and she spent all the grocery and milk money on herself that night.

- A lady was so vain she spent the last of her money knowing she wouldn't get anymore for another whole month. So frustrated about the way she looked she went ahead and got her hair doo. But the next day didn't have gas money to take the child to its doctor's appointment.

- Another Missy sold all her food stamps to buy drugs and had no feelings about future consequences because she was numb inside. So the hungry crying kids and the empty cupboards didn't faze her one bit. Because of pure selfishness. A tool that the enemy uses in many people's lives today.

- A husband intentionally goes out drinking every night. Gambling away all the bill money. Then the family gets threatened with an eviction notice because he lost the rent money.

People these are real issues of life. But God has nothing to do with your issues here. You have self-inflicted yourself with selfishness and God wants to give you a spirit of Power, Love and a Sound Mind. He has not given any of us a spirit of Fear.

Granted if all the following above is happening in your life, there is no sense of peace.

So what are you going to do about it? We're going to use our *simple sense strategy methods* to bring success into our lives. Replacing selfishness with love is the key.

Which we'll go over in more detail in **Success Method #3**

But look right now at the **"L"** in the Word Help! Referring back to the Success Method #2 HELP = Here on Earth to Love People.

If you're loving people then selfishness has no room in your life. Then and only then will you thrive in life, ministry, business and career endeavors. Never leave your children scratching for sustenance, food and nurture. It's a woman's, and mother's responsibility to nurture the family through love and prayer.

If a mother has said in her actions "I'll deal with these issues in my household later, or if she finds herself giving the baby water in the place of milk or formula. When it's the vitamins and nutrients that child needs. Then you can plainly see where her deeper love lies. (It's all about herself)! This is a very ugly thing.

Your greater purpose with being successful stems from your life portraying love in such a way that brings wholeness to others.

By using the second - Success Method #2 HELP - to pull your life upward. And then business and life will not be as usual, but as God wills. Extraordinary!

EXAMPLES OF SELFISH ATTRIBUTES CONTINUED

The extremely wealthy

So we've used some examples of misses, ladies, and women who may be on welfare or have lower income households. And we saw how the actions they were taking with selfishness caused them to slowly chip away at the building of their own homes and families.

But the strategies in this book fit all people. Be encouraged to know that Jesus Christ has paid a price for all people to be free, successful, and happy in life. It doesn't matter which side of the track you've come from. Everyone needs to come into this success of life. And it starts with Jesus Christ. That's your starting point.

Now, continuing with our scenario examples of SELFISHNESS:

Look at the extremely wealthy woman who has all the resources and monetary benefits to do whatever she wants, whenever she wants.

Let's say… she does not Work on a 9 to 5 job. She's a stay at home mom. But she gets all her needs met. All her goodies of life are coming through her husband, who's a millionaire.

This doesn't make the millionaire wife any different from the low income mom. It only puts the rich wife in a different status quo relating to the worlds standards. But in Gods eyes it doesn't make her any different as far as being a human being that God trusts to be responsible. Why?

Because success is not about money – at least not in the way we think. The problem here is that society thinks success has all to do with money. (Remember I talked about selfish mindsets) well here's some more stinking thinking.

For instance: when you find the rich person turning their nose up at the poor. It's not the homeless man or poor bum on skid row that stinks. It's your mindset that does. This literature is about changing negative mindsets so that you'll think differently about yourself and money. It's about using biblical principles so much that your bones reek of doing what's right and good.

If you answered NO to my question I asked above, about the two women being different, then you're on the track of where I'm going with this mindset scenario.

NO, the wealthy woman is not any different than the woman of little means.

I didn't say they were the same. I said they're no different in their mindset. Obviously, the wealthy woman has more money and can afford to do more and spend more however she chooses. This most likely makes her just a little more dangerous. What is her motive for spending? What's behind the mask she wears? Is it loneliness, dissatisfaction, hurt or pain? Think about it.

Why is she running up the credit cards to record debt? Splurging on shopping sprees every month? Or shopping till she drops and eating out daily at a bank-breaking price?

You still see the ugly guise of SELFISHNESS raise its head once again. Just as before with the low to no income person. It can't be helped without Christ in our life. By nature we all were born selfish. But with a new nature - that of Christ we can change that.

I know that there are a lot of smart women out there…

And this book: "Biblical Business Bones" is specifically written to help those who are open to encouragement, motivation and are pliable enough to receive something fresh. It's for those who are ready to view successfulness from another woman's experience and Gods perspective.

Let's face it; none of us were called to save anybody. Christ does that. But on the other hand, we were called with a purpose to be somebody who could and would HELP! =

Here on Earth to Love People. The bible says to treat your neighbor as you treat yourself. Now tell me how can I love my neighbor if I don't love myself, or if I'm hurting myself? Inflicting confusion into my home by fighting with my husband about how I'm spending money and so forth?

Remember: my job is to keep refreshing this until you get it into your mindset, reflect upon a truth and do what'll set you free.

Using the strategy of HELP is about what Jesus did during his whole time on earth. He didn't pass people up because he was so anointed, or too good to help them. But on the contrary, he saw through eyes of compassion and helped all he could - those who wanted it.

So if Jesus is our example for success in life and business. Then we have the greatest keys anybody could ever hope to find. And that's to LOVE - First God, Secondly you, (self) and third mankind.

You're probably thinking, well to love myself means I have to go out and do something nice for myself so I can feel better about myself. No it doesn't. That's the way a carnal mind would think. But if you've looked into the Good Book – the Bible, your mind has been transformed by the Words of Christ. It hasn't stayed the same as before. Your mindset can't sit in unconformity or stay parked at worldly and carnal.

The world says oh I'm feeling depressed and down so I'll go spend lots of money on me. I think I'll get my hair done, buy a new expensive dress. Stop in for a pedi and manni. And guys you don't say much of anything. You just get depressed and go buy a new boat, motorcycle or truck. Rich woman, you accept an invitation to a high society luncheon that you know you shouldn't be paying $5,000 - $10,000 dollars for the nicely laid out little bit of food they're serving. What's up with that picture?

Or you'll go hang out with your click - chicks. You know the ones you only support because they support your business - the ones who look down on others saying… "If you're not in our "elite business click" then you don't fit! Wow! Are you for real? This is so unreal; there are a lot of masks being worn out there. And although you know the world can't see them. Christ can.

Woman you thought you had to make a sacrifice, when the baby only had one diaper left. And you decided to get that hair-doo, just so you could look good for your man. And you're saying to yourself… 'If that isn't loving myself - then I don't know what is.'

Again, I say WOW! Can you see that the motive and mindset here still boils down to SELFISHNESS? And right about now I'm getting tired of that word and you should be also. So let's deal with it. Let's kick it in the butt!

You saw earlier on… the meaning of the word Selfish. And now all you have to do is flip that coin over and find a little inscription on the other side: called LOVE. We mentioned it earlier as well.

LOVE is your key to kicking Selfishness in the behind and getting it out of your mind.

LOVE will go further than your eyes can see. Further than your money can spend. And if you do decide to spend Love like you spend money that you have or may not have, your investment and return will be greatly abundant, which brings us to our third Success Method.

SUCCESS METHOD #3 (Love)
LOVE = Living Out Vital Efforts

When I first set out to write this book and put together the strategies that I've used in my own life. When I looked at this word Love I pondered it. Because being a minister I've seen love from so many aspects of life.

But for this particular book, which is written basically to help women who are not quite up there yet, in their thinking. I came up with the acronym – to fit my business model of love for the Business Minded Woman.

This turned out to be: Living out Vital Efforts.

So my first question to each of you is:

ARE YOUR EFFORTS FILLED WITH WHAT MATTERS?

 What's vital to your family and those attached to you in business, career, life and ministry? If not, you need to check your aim, drive and intent. It's so easy for each of us to forget the big picture:

- The fact that each one – reaches one,

- The truth that we need each other

- The command to love one another

Some may even think my little scenario about the welfare mom and extremely wealthy wife was a little over the top... Whatever you thought, its real life! And that's Ok. I know who I am and why I do what I do. It's to help others. He brought me from some of these places so I can live out my testimony of praise.

None the less, I had to draw a practical picture that would take us to a point that would get us to this page of our discussion. If starting with a negative will eventually bring you to a positive, then it's a good thing that I've done.

See I already checked my motives before I even started the book. Know that I love you and want you to do more than well, more than good. I want for you to be the best that you should in your success with life. God originally intended this for you. And my heart just wants what His does.

So In the LOVE Success Method #3 – we must first know what the Golden Rule is in order to inherit the Golden Key to Success.

So many people strive for money. Then run after it with all their might. But that's not the golden key. God never once told anyone to run so hard after money that they forget about the important things or people. In fact that very golden rule was the teaching of Jesus that you should treat others as you would like them to treat you. Remember if you're not up then how can you reach down to pull someone else up?

Read it here: found in Luke 10:27 -

He answered, "You shall love the Lord your God with all your heart, with all your soul, with all your strength, and with your entire mind; and your neighbor as yourself."

It's not a careless mannered thing we do. And again, understand that we cannot do this loving thing outside of Christ and without

God's help. God is the only one with a love pure enough for you and me to LOVE! Or Live Out Vital Efforts.

HOW TO GET THERE

You can come into this pure love by allowing Christ Jesus to be Lord of your life.

You do that by partaking of His divine nature through the conversion of grace.

I hope you are starting to see these simple sense strategies.

That Love will become easy because Christ has already done the hard part of the work. God has set forth his kindness and love toward all mankind.   But do understand that even so, you have a small part to do…That's the EFFORT part you must take.

It's going to take some effort on your part before you ever see your seeds come to the light. Why do you think I kept getting back up when I failed at business? Why do you think I kept researching and trying to find my niche until I did? With God's help of course. It's because you must do something today to plan your tomorrow.

I shared earlier how that I sunk quite a bit of money into trying to do several types of businesses several different times. I've sold bold beauty products, consumer products and services and gifts and more. I've personally invested thousands of dollars into business.

God knew my motives from the beginning. It was to obey the word by putting my hands to something. The Word of God tells me that whatever I put my hands to will be blessed. That's a promise key from the bible I'll always believe in. The bible also tells me that without faith it's impossible to please God. And that Faith without Works is dead. So if Faith is an action word, that means I had to make an Effort to do something, right?

Now you're getting it. I did something because I believed by doing so, I could be at a place where I could help someone else. And all this was true to a degree.

Before you go out and try to do business on your own put the following strategies in place first.

- Get a plan, vision, strategy and put it on paper
- Find a coach, mentor or do your research, and get the resources you need
- Don't' forget how to be a success at the risk of becoming successful

We're speaking about LOVE: living out vital efforts.

For example: It's not vital that you strive to get rich and forget to live your life. Are you still with me? God may just be telling you like he told me, to shut the front door. Stop grazing your front lawn and quit gazing at your neighbors. Some of you may be looking over at your neighbor's house coveting their material goods.

You and your neighbor are not the same. Let God show you your talent and gift so you can use them for success in life. My word to you is to come on in to Christ.

He may be speaking to you to go turn over some soil in the backyard of your heart. So He can continue to nurture the seeds of success that were planted there from the beginning of the foundation of time. When this seed is ready, if it has not already bloomed with you and from you. It will bring with it life!

Life that causes you to live on purpose. Making sure everything you do is VITAL and important. Urgent and worthy of every EFFORT.

© Ralph Waldo Emerson once said: "enthusiasm is the mother of Effort, and without it nothing great was ever achieved.

You want something to be enthused about? Let the Lord Jesus show you His love. That'll surely bring enthusiasm. And then your capacity to give and help will become large.

The word enthusiasm simply means: (keen interest and excitement!)

 Let me endorse Business Bones

First off what do I mean when I speak or talk about Business?

Going back to the testimony of my life with business ventures. You've heard it. There I was spending dollars, precious time and efforts were definitely put forth to be a success I felt deep down within me I was supposed to be.

Was I wrong to do such a thing? Did I make mistakes? Let me answer those.

First I was not wrong in what I did as I said before. God honors you when you put forth effort to move out in faith and be somebody better. If you're doing it with right motive. To make the world you live in a better place. So to speak.

Secondly, did I make some mistakes? Most certainly YES! I'm transparent enough to let you know I did. And we all do. We're human and that's why. So my focus with the book is to share with you a bit of knowledge that may help you bypass some of the mistakes I've made.

I am a business person who plays football on a field with many other team members. And as a player I continue to learn more. But today in 'Biblical Business Bones' I intend to continue to help you as a coach. By offering a few strategies toward your younger success. Kind of like a mother motivating her younger daughter.

When we look at Business we see it being done all the time. In many different places. All over the global world and in every episode of life. As we know business is what makes our world thrive and It's how the economy survives. This was my purpose for the book. To bring a fresh new approach and a God perspective relating to business as God would want you and me to do it as a Christian.

The word business means: an occupation, profession, or trade. So when we think about a man or woman going to work. They are taking care of business. And even when a mother cleans her house, she's doing the business of her daily affairs. When a child goes to school - his business is to learn how to function with others of his own age.

Down to when a baby poops her diaper, she just took care of business with no worries at all. Why? Because she knows that shortly thereafter, mommy is going to take care of business when she quickly holds her breath to change that smelly diaper.

So these are just some of the ways business is being done from all walks of life. Again we see that business is all around us being done in all kinds of ways, forms and fashions. Which brings us to our Next simple sense strategy called BEING

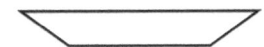

SUCCESS METHOD #4 (Being)

BEING = Best Ever In Necessary Gestures

Notice I put in bold caption and underscored The word Being above. In order to bring out this method you must realize that there's Value in doing business with others. Or in serving them. It means whatever I Do in my life, business and ministry I'll remember it should always be about...Putting forth the Best Ever in my Necessary Gestures.

In other words, your best foot forward for family, work, church, business and community.

And whenever we're doing life this way, with Love and not selfishly, God gets the Kudos and you'll get the success, money and abundance.

Whenever you start being who God created you to be you'll start living and stop barely making it.

What's GESTURE?

The use of such movements to express thought, emotion, etc. Any action, courtesy, communication, intended for effect or as a formality; considered expression; demonstration: Example: a gesture of friendship.

In other words, it's what I do in my world around me that makes all the difference. What am I expressing to others while I'm out there moving among them in business, ministry, work, church etc? My very body language says something to them. Do you show courtesy to those who serve you and whom you serve? This again is a type of honor that only God has required of mankind towards one another.

What about my communication with my business world? Do I really hear the dis-satisfied customer? The pleased client? The Instructions of my mentor/coach/trainer or teacher? Think about it. Then go and do it, be it, act it out. Putting forth the Best Ever in all your Gestures towards a world that's forgotten about integrity, honor and humility.

In order to communicate you must start a dialogue. Remember this; God didn't call anybody to be alone. If he wanted that, then he would have put you here on earth by yourself. Wow – how lonely would that have been? No one to listen to. No one to teach us anything. No challenges to grow and be better…you get my drift.

So go out and find people who are going to help you in your movement.

Example:

The Gestures you make are going to happen in your everyday life.

And they are just some of the actions, movements, communications and demonstrations that'll bring the success you're looking for. Remember we are not talking about killing yourself over any business and ministry. Neither am I talking about running over others to get to success. I'm not speaking about stressing yourself out over pursuing money. But I am talking about using the ELEVEN Success Methods to create priority and balance in life while you're working out your business plans. So please, don't talk yourself out of doing something so simple - that many have overlooked. These Methods work.

Beware... 'Success is found in doing what others are not doing. Or have taken for granted.'

So many people are talking about How To Get Filthy Rich these days. But that's not what this book is about. This book is about being successful in life. Being whole in yourself. Not forgetting who your true source is. And treating others fair in business. All these components compiled together bring the fullness of joy and contentment, which many are seeking. Your Joy is not in your money. It may make you happy but money can't buy love or true joy. Only the Lord and Savior can give those benefits.

There is a big difference between Joy and happiness. There's a big difference between busy and balance. People are most happy when they have money and they should be grateful. King Solomon said in the Good Book - the Bible... A feast is made for laughter, and wine maketh merry: but money answereth all things. Ecclesiastes 10:19.

But if that money runs out, then what? Does the money control the character of who we are? For some it does. It depends on what a person has deposited on the inside of their life. Get it? I hope you understand that money is a good thing and God wants you and me to have plenty of it to help others and build his kingdom.

To give balance to this section of the talk in "Biblical Business Bones" Let's look at TWELVE biblical principles about money. This will help you with balance in your business, ministry, career and life.

12 THINGS ABOUT MONEY THAT WILL BRING THE

PROPER KIND OF SUCCESS IF FOLLOWED:

FOUNDATION SCRIPTURE:

The Good Book Bible says…in (Ecclesiastes 10:19) …

"MONEY ANSWERETH ALL THINGS!"

- Money determines the Standard of Life

- Money represents Wealth, Prosperity and Our Well Being

- Money gives Peace, Joy and Fulfillment

- Money is needed to do Good Works

- Money is needed to do the Ministry or to Serve God

- Money belongs to God

- Money is available to the Children of God without any limits

- Money can be multiplied through Giving and Investment

- Money should be Properly Managed

- Money should not be our Goal or God

- Money and wealth are available in this World in Abundance

- Money should be used to Fulfill God's Purposes

Now as I said, God does want you to have money and be a success, but not at the risk of losing all. The biggest thing we see happen when people aren't ready for larger amounts of money is they forget the principles above. God doesn't what us to serve money or put it as priority over Him, our families or others. Don't have twisted motives. Don't be like the people who are running out daily to make the big bucks. Chasing after the things they think is going to bring them money and happiness. These same people have failed to optimize their talents in a proper way. This brings me back to the importance of priority.

Priority in my Gestures: How's your family doing? Are you leaving them out of your priorities or are you including them into your life. Who you are and what you do. Honoring them by making sure they are in the right lineup. Don't' be that woman that starts a business and then forget about the house, kids, hubby and others. Don't forget about your health and life either. But ask God to come help you line up your day. We don't always know how to do that - In fact, I'd say 100% of the time we just don't know how to do life. But He loves us and he's got your back even when we all get it wrong.

Misplaced Priority: Means I'll try to juggle a million and one things trying to press into my success.

Balanced Priority: Means I'll take the one thing that I see working and optimize and maximize that. Get it to working for me and see results with it first. Before stressing over other things that most likely are not going to fit into my plans period.

RECAP SUMMARY:

Let me recap for a moment what we've learned so far about simple sense strategies that will take us into being successful in our business, life and ministry. Particularly when we rehearse them into our daily affairs.

Remember we spoke earlier about the backyard. So, I just want to remind those of you who may have just happen to find your golden key in that back yard, whatever type of business or ministry it is. You can look at these Success Methods and Simple Sense Strategies as ROCKS…You need a rock because it's supportive and strong. It holds up the foundation of whatever it is you've planted.

We've dug up the weeds of selfishness that may have been rooted deep. We re-laid the foundation by putting in some good textured soil (into our hearts) called love.

<u>**REFRESHER**</u>

SUCCESS METHOD #1 Ways = With All Your Support

No man or woman is an island. You can't remain isolated and succeed.

- I need you

- You need me

SUCCESS METHOD #2 Help = Here on Earth to Love People

- Selfishness no longer binds or blinds me
- I'm Free to love you and help you, if you let me

SUCCESS METHOD #3 Love = Living out Vital Efforts

- Are the efforts I take vital, urgent or important?
- Do I have the capacity to live those out properly?

SUCCESS METHOD #4 Being = Best Ever in Necessary Gestures

- Value systems are crucial - My best gestures move me forward.

Next we're going to talk about something that a lot of women have not done yet. Some of you even struggle with this. But be encouraged to know that Christ wants you to imagine yourself as He does. Complete and Perfect. That's it. Nothing else doing.

Side Note: If you've worked your Success Method # 3 (Love) you are ready to learn about this next step called "acceptance."

Acceptance is just another one of those simple little strategies that's going to take easy efforts of implementation. In other words, Ladies this is going to take easy strides in causing you success if you act upon this Method.

SUCCESS METHOD #5 (Acceptance)

ACCEPTANCE = The Assurance that Gives Life

You may be asking what acceptance has to do with the business bones of success. Momentarily, I'll let you in on that secret. But first let's get the full understanding of what acceptance is.

ACCEPTANCE: means …The act of taking or receiving something offered. A favorable reception or approval. The act of assenting or believing.

When I started to take a look at that word, "acceptance" the first thing that came to mind were the words… past, future, and present. With "'Acceptance" one must get over their personal fears before they are able to move forward. Example: if you failed at some type of business venture or task in life. Weather in your past or recently, then chances is without a doubt it setup a mindset of failure causing you to stall. Or become hindered from moving into your now (present) and later (future).

To execute this SUCCESS METHOD – Acceptance, you must become ok with letting go of the past failures and things that brought about the spirit of fear. It's just the opposite of Faith. What are you willing to accept? Are you willing to move forward to the best life you could ever have dreamed or imagined? Well you sure can't do that living I n fear. You must let your faith stretch the levels of acceptance and push past the past that has limited you from stepping into your future harvest of blessings.

Look at the two scenarios below: They're two types of acceptance you'll need to feel good about and step into upon operating your business.

Self acceptance vs. Personal fear

Social acceptance vs. Public fear

You must accept yourself for who God created you to be.

You must realize you have value that lies somewhere inside you. 'God didn't make no junk' as the old cliché says. You must be willing to recognize the fact that you're also valued as a human being. Valued by someone, somewhere, sometimes. Once you realize your self-worth you can sell anything to your market. Having this kind of attitude helps you believe that no matter what you've put out there as a product or service, your confidence in the hard work you've done something with your resources will bring the results. So have faith in who you are and what you're doing.

Repeat it daily:

I raise my personal level of self-esteem - self confidence and self awareness by being confident in the Lord and what He's said about me and my business venture (s). I am a success in anything I do and everything I put my hands to.

You must study diligently to know who you are first and what your product, goods and services will be later. Then and only then will you realize this principle, (Acceptance) is The Assurance that Gives Life.

You say how? Well, faith in who you are, who God is and what you can do is very mind- freeing. And anything that's free is liberating. It's a sure thing. Its life as he intended.

Remember the front yard and backyard scenario? Well your personal treasure just may be in the front yard. I'm not putting you in a box here. I just shared with you the true life story about my success and satisfaction being found in my own back yard. This example doesn't in any way; tie you to either the front or backyard.

I just want to say wherever you find your treasure - The key is to accept it! Surely you'll be able to do that, after you've learned to accept the fact that sometimes you may fail again. The key here is to never stop short of your dream. When you find it…that hidden treasure it'll be well worth it. So keep at it and be willing to first see it, recognize it, flow with it, and allow it to bring you your success. You do this by embracing the gift, the treasure, the talent, the skill, the ability and faculties God has shown you in your personal life. All of that is what ACCEPTANCE is all about.

Before you spend another dime. Before you use another minute of your precious time trying to figure out what business you'll do. I want you to first sit down and take inventory of yourself. Think about it, and think hard. Then ask yourself "WHO AM I" then ask God for the wisdom you need to understand how to put who you are into your business, your job, your ministry and your life. Then once you've got peace about this, you can move forward.

Also, another resource to help you in this step forward with your acceptance is a small but powerful 113 page book I've written, called *"Little Purple Book of I AMS.* You can get it at our website at the end of this book. The book was written to help encourage people to change negative attitudes. If one does the ten day challenge they'll see their altitude has changed because of their attitude change.

I don't know of anybody who went in a positive, good or successful way by being negative. But thousands upon thousands of people have accomplished their goals by looking up and moving forward with a positive attitude. By focusing, staying on track and accentuating the positive things. Think about it. God's book says... Whatever is good and perfect comes down to us from God our Father, James 1:17. This is how he made you. Acceptance is about speaking back to yourself the good things that are supposed to be in your life. If you hear yourself saying them, then you'll believe them. Then you'll change the direction you're going in. Especially, if it's a downward, destructive, habitual negative direction.

Now, about the resourceful tools, my motive here is not to drop in a sales plug, though it may look like that's what I just did with my Little Purple Book. But I'm so confident that if you use the book you'll be soaring on high in your business in no time.

See my faith in you is to believe you want better. And the confidence in myself to believe I can help you. Again, this method of success is called: HELP = Here On Earth to Love Don't you know that if I love God, I'll help you - and if I help you, I'm obeying God? HOW? By simply using my skill set He's equipped me with.

I realize I've been loved and favored by God to find my way. So now I pay that blessing forward to you. So get the book and start living the UP life. Even through your storms, you can be UP on the inside of your spirit - When you execute God's Words about you.

Anyway, back to our Strategy of Acceptance:

Once a person realizes ACCEPTANCE - it breeds love and freedom. When you come to this integral part of your journey you are on the right road to lead you through the portal of success.

You must have the way of ACCEPTANCE - bleeding through your blood, all the way down to your BONES. That's your life. And without blood pumping in life, as you know, a person is dead!

When you began to deal with your own Acceptance, you're going to start feeling the amazing things inside your bones that you can do. And you'll move forward with exuberance hardly able to wait to do them as well. This is what you'll free yourself to.

HOW DO YOU DO IT?

Well I'm so glad you asked. Below are four easy steps you'll need to take before you can ever master becoming a success in life. Please don't skip them because they are guaranteed to help you.

Easy Steps:

- Recognize you can't figure it out on your own – ask for help, then research and pursue more knowledge about what you're doing.

- Ask God for wisdom and understanding he'll have you to see…

- Make God your Business and Ministry Consultant or Partner…

- Make up your mind to stick to your goals even if you don't see quick results.

Then you will be successful.

Before looking at our sixth method of success, I realize that there are many success gurus out there who've written good books on business. But I base my guarantees on the Word of God - Which is a great trustworthy source for blessings and wealth. When we put God first he'll put us first. Since we're fallible and God isn't we need his help all the time. But if you fail in what you're doing its good to know you have someone like God right there to pick you up, brush you off, and send you on your way again. With Him you'll have the strength to try to raise that dream up again.

Use the blank Note Space below to work out your plan of action, Organize, Strategize. Write something down about your business you'll take steps with today:

SUCCESS METHOD #6 (Honesty)
HONESTY= Holding onto earnest sincere truths

In success method six we look at the word honesty. In basics of life and business, we all know that honesty should be the best policy. At least it's the one thing we should practice daily and cling to as much as possible. People want to know they can trust others. But humans will still take a risk at getting hurt or even being taken by a scam because that's in every human beings nature. I want to stress here that to do a business you must have a character of truth and sincerity for your customers and clients. Don't ever let your business model start with a lie or it'll end up there.

The negative benefits are:

If we are not honest and genuine people of integrity in our business of life, we will eventually come to a halt. Be put out of business and may even burn some bridges behind us with hurt and shame. God has said in his word that we can't mock Him. He's watching our every move. Whatever we sow or plant, we'll reap the same. So if you plant crooked, shady, cheating behaviors you'll reap this kind of harvest in your business. And that my friend is not business success.

My word to you is to always exemplify honesty and then you'll show forth a spirit of excellence. Just like Daniel did in the bible. He was a man of wisdom and knowledge and he feared God and prayed three times a day. But there were those who were jealous of him because he was favored and had success as well. So they went to the king and lied on him and got him into trouble. But the bible says he only kept to his character of integrity and honesty and for it the king later called him forth and addressed him as a man of excellence.

When the king asked Daniel if he had disobeyed his command to not pray. Daniel didn't lie and say "no" to the king, but instead told the King the truth. That he had to go on praying because he had to obey God first. But he never once dishonored the king in any of this. Daniel's holding to the truth during that moment may have caused him to be thrown into the lion's den, but the King's heart was broken because he had to do such a thing to such a man as Daniel. Plus he wasn't alone there in the lion's den and God shut the lions mouth as well.

Never believe that telling a lie is best. In the long run it's not. In fact when you tell the truth the benefits are... as I said earlier on when dealing with the Success Method of Acceptance... truth frees a person. Did you know that it takes more strength and energy to hold to a lie than it does to just tell the truth and be an honest person? Lies only breed negative. For example: when you lie you tie a yoke or burden around your neck and soul. Then the enemy causes guilt to set in, along with all other kinds of evil. The better life consists of you using the easy simply strategy method of HONESTY = holding onto earnest sincere truths. Which brings about health, wealth, happiness and success.

Some of you may have been scammed a few times, just as I have. That's because many have not been honesty in their dealings. But instead they've been misleading by committing fraud and manipulation in order to get their own business to succeed. And it was all about themselves and their personal gain. But we've already learned about five other business methods that will keep you from falling into these types of traps.

There have been many a man and woman who have sold their souls for the almighty dollar. Breeding in the spirit of Greed. Remember, greed is the opposite of true success. The bible tells us to fret not ourselves because of what the evil man is doing. It says this man's life can only come to misery and failure in the end.

You ask about the person who's working and trying their best to be fair and do good, and you're wondering why some of them have not hit the jack pot yet, so to speak. I have an encouraging word for you. That when you are an honest person you'll be successful in everyday life period. But there is another Success Method that ties with the Method of Honesty and that's success Method # 7 – it's called Qualification.

SUCCESS METHOD #7 (Qualification)
QUALIFY = Equipped to Compete

When we consider this word we find that It means to provide with proper or necessary skills, knowledge, and credentials, to make one competent: as if to qualify oneself for a job. It also means to be fitted. To get authority, license, and power, by fulfilling required conditions. To have the ability.

Let's look at the ability part of qualification. I want to see what the bible has to say about our ability. Our business is His business and His business is the concern of each one of you.

Don't worry if you feel inadequate to do the job. God hasn't called you because you could do it in yourself anyway. Remember, He gives us the tools we need to get the job started and completed. We must have our faith and trust in him to qualify us. Because He's the one who put the desire there anyway in the first place.

So, In order to visualize your qualification of doing your business or ministry, you must know that you've been destined to be great or do something more with your life. Don't just settle for status quo. Too many people do that. Don't become a statistic of just waiting around for something to happen. You move out and He'll shine the light of where next you should put your foot on that path.

All business models have shown that if you're tired of getting the same old results you must change what you're doing. Oh yeah, what is it that you're doing? Are you moving up the latter in your career? Are you growing your ministry and church? Are you making connections and building life partners through your business. Are you inspiring others through your authoritative gifts or given talents?

The bible says to stir up the gift that is within you. That gift was given to be a blessing to others. So get started.

These are just questions for you to think about. Don't forget about what's on the front or back lawn! Remember you must expect to find something when you look out the door. You must then prepare to run with it. Have you established your plans or ideas of success yet?

Education is a key to success. The more you know the further you can go. So educate yourself frequently. The world is constantly changing and so are new found ways to do something better. The world moves so fast that if we aren't enhancing our knowledge weekly, practically daily, we'll miss out on some things that could be very beneficial to our life, business and ministry. It's always about "what's working now." We can't go into our future with something that worked ten years ago. We need the fresh and the new. I'm sure you've hear it said...in business we must be on the 'The cutting edge.' Or we've got to be 'razor sharp.' And now it's the latest ... 'laser sharp.' You get what I'm saying. So education always rock!

Educate your staff, workers and others: this is called dropping the mantle. You want to free up your time to do more of the things that will cause the business to continue to grow. Give the worker bees the inside work and you continue to educate others, connect to other clients and customers, who in turn will help your business only grow. Then those that you educate will duplicate what you're doing in business. This will also make your work twice as easy and much better.

This next success method is about improving your existing life's situations? If you want to do that and you're serious about it...then you'll move forward and take a step to invest in your venture. Therefore, this strategy is called... Investment!

SUCCESS METHOD #8 (Investment(s)
INVESTMENTS = Seeds

What does it mean to invest in something?

First, what is investing? Investing is "the act of committing money or capital to an endeavor (a business, project, real estate, etc.) with the expectation of obtaining an additional income or profit."

Investment Strategies

Investing: in a long term approach with a specific goal. For example, you may want to invest into your own retirement or your kid's college with some of the money you make from your business. Both of these can have a predetermined date and targeted dollar amount.

Saving: is different from investing because there's really no risk with it. After your business grows financially you may chose to start saving short term or long term. It just depends on your savings goals. You can guarantee some savings just by using a money market or CD ladder savings accounts. This is a great way to preserve capital.

Trading: Then again, you may want to look into some day trading, as ways for short term investments and money making. This would and could be done with stocks with an intention of owning for possibly a day, month or one year.

Just know that when you start to make money you need to find ways to preserve some and make more. This is called being a good steward. Money is funny. You could have a lot of today and if you didn't respect money, it could be gone tomorrow. All the keys given are effective ways to keep your money flowing back into your business and life. You must sow both ways. Naturally and spiritually.

It's no secret that your investments are called your seeds. If a man or woman sows seed or plants a garden, are they not to expect some kind of harvest in return?

In this case, if you're wondering if your business secrets are safe, then I'd have to say no! We cannot deny the principle of seedtime and harvest here. You are guaranteed one hundred percent to receive some kind of a return on your investments.

Investing is just another type of planting and trusting: look here at scripture:

"But this I say: He who sows sparingly will also reap sparingly, and he who sows bountifully will also reap bountifully" (2

Corinthians 9:6). Your sowing decides your reaping. You order your harvest in advance by the seeds you plant.

Other Investing Strategies: ARE…Stock, Inventory, Products, Goods and Services.

What type of business is it: Are you going to have to stock supplies and inventory? Are you offering Services? Or selling Goods? Whichever it is, you'll need to look at another aspect of investing.

For instance:

You must Investment in your stock & Inventory – products, goods and services.

What does your customer or client need? Start investing in that on a small scale first, and then grow from there. Look for product on sale and stock up. Do you have a warehouse, garage, or storage unit? Use it to house your goods until you're ready to sell.

Invest in your thought processes and mindsets. Daily put the dream before you of what you expect your business to look like. Then see it, hear yourself declaring it and see it already established. This helps tons. If you've let go of your dream, it's time to dream again. Start today rebuilding a respect for your business goals and dreams.

Remember these simple keys to success:
- Get clarity on what you want from life

- Understand where it is you want to go in life

- Start speaking what you expect to see

- Rule life and don't let life ruin you and your family

- Chart your course and start creating your dreams of success

- Learn all you can and pour back out towards others.

Then tangible good results will follow.

SUCCESS METHOD #9 (Balance)

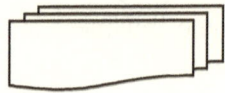

BALANCE = Brought Forward to End Well

If you're a new business owner there are a few things you must take control of. Namely, juggling the balance act of work and family life. When you learn to achieve this balance you'll become better for it.

First I want to say you're not to think of life as some kind of get rich or die trying syndrome. But commonsense tells us we must take care of self in order to have the strength to even do a business/ministry. That being said. Don't forget to take care of the following six areas of who you are before moving forward with your dream of business and / or ministry.

- Family,

- Business, Ministry

- My Mental Mind

- My Physical Body

- My Social Life

- My Spiritual Involvements

Take a survey of where you are with these various arenas of life. Take note of which ones are getting the most attention and sucking up huge amounts of time? Put your live into a priority perspective and keep a balance here. For Example: Don't substitute your rest and exercise for making a quick buck. Don't neglect your children or let resentment come in between you and your spouse because you're so gong-ho about your business. I've heard others say in the past, this was OK, as long as they made it up later. I don't agree with those others, because chances are they won't get to make it up later. Don't sacrifice the preciousness of your family; by thinking what you're doing is for them.

All they need is a little bit of your time. Especially moms with small children.

Do the workout regime that releases the stress and gives you the vitality to continue on in your business. Take time with the Word of God in meditation to renew your mindsets. Spend time being social. Put some emphasis on your being involved with your church and spiritual groups; volunteer with charities and giving back. This all has to do with self-care! Plus this is where success lies. The more balanced you become the better you become, Amen!

Though hard work and perseverance are the key elements to being a success, you must always remember to keep a balance between what you're doing and building your family. You must look at all the perspectives of your Success Formula so you don't lose the balance that'll help you in the long run to win.

Decency, Honesty, and Modesty are three more keys that come to mind when I'm considering my balance. Never overdo a thing in hopes of becoming rich. Anything that's not been tested, tried, or characterized is not good. This is how you keep on top. By checking with your motives for wanting to be a success and have money.

There's nothing wrong with money except the love of it. We are not to love money so much that we'll become charlatans who seek after others in hopes of taking advantage of them. Solomon once said... "Money answers all things." But Jesus said as well... "The Love of Money had a root of evil." It's what you want to do with the money and where your heart's motive is that'll determine your success.

Let's look at four more perspectives we must use as a strategy to keep balance with what we're building with our business and / or ministry.

PERSPECTIVE # 1

- Training & Self-Improvement

In your business model, if you have others working for you, they'll have to be trained with the same principles and values you want to uphold in your business.

Just as you've sought to improve yourself to be a success, you must pass the baton down to them in order to bring them up in their thinking and actions toward the business organization. The most important thing with this strategy is to be open to change and continue learning for both...Yourself and Your workers. And remember, the knowledge you implement is the powerful key to any success in life.

PERSPECTIVE # 2

- Inner Process

To be successful with your business model, again, you'll have to spend some time as a leader, if it's a ministry or as a entrepreneur if it's a business, getting to know how well your own business is running.   You must spend amply amounts of time going over the products and services to see if they are working for the client, customer and or vendors. Your mission when you got started should have been to be all you could be in a good way, so that you would become equipped to help serve the customer. If you haven't already, you should spend some time getting to know what it'll take to not just sell the customer, but to please your customer. In some cases this is called AECR = Accelerated – Excellent – Customer – Relations. When you start to become intimate about your business and its products you'll start to see major success with repeat customers. It's just that simple.

PERSPECTIVE # 3

- Customers

Never fail to realize the customer's needs first. After all, they are the people who keep all of us in business. Without these human beings any economy would suffer. In perspective number three – concerning your business. A great value of importance must be put on the individual who has come to buy from your market, or your place of business. As a business owner your relationships with them is what counts most. Focus on them by listening to what it is they need and want. To run a true business and be successful at it, you must be a servant – leader. Leading and serving at the same time. Don't make the mistake of ever thinking you can be successful without the customer, client or vendor. Their satisfactions are leading indicators to your success. Remember also, our customers are the people who keep us focused with balance. They keep us honorable as we honor them. They keep us humble as well.

You did not go into your business to decline later. You didn't start your ministry to just give up or fold over later either! Remember, God has given you the ability to succeed. You've been equipped and made competent to fix, provide, mend or help. So communicate these strategies into your organization with positive vigor and you'll reap what you've sown.

PERSPECTIVE # 4

- Money

It can't be stressed enough, that your reason for making money should be so you can bless and help someone else. You saw this principle in the section where we spoke about God's agenda for money. During the process of building your dream sometimes you'll be taking others up with you. And at other times, you'll need to set-in that financial stability first. I can't heal someone if I'm broken. I can't feed someone if I don't have an over abundance supply for me, mine and others. I think you get what I'm saying here. Then you'll be more able to bring others you're including in your plans, business and life into the mix.

As we all know traditionally, it takes money to make money. So this perspective would always be one to factor in. However you're choosing to support your business and/or ministry you must have some kind of funding. Money plans. This is priority with the right perspective. Always think large even if you have to be realistic, as I was. You usually start small and grow from there. On the other hand, don't forget to add in the risk factors of losing a little money. Don't leave anything out of this process. Then you'll set yourself up as a winner.

SUCCESS METHOD #10 (Research)

RESEARCH = Just What IT IS!

Diligent and systematic inquiry or investigation

Into a subject in order to discover or revise facts,

Theories, applications, etc.:

Market research is any organized effort to gather information about markets or customers. It is a very important component of business strategy. The term is commonly interchanged with marketing research; however, expert practitioners may wish to draw a distinction, in that marketing research is concerned specifically about marketing processes, while market research is concerned specifically with markets.

Market Research is a key factor to get advantage over competitors. Market research provides important information to identify and analyze the market need, market size and competition.

You must find out who you're competing with so you'll be smarter in your market. Doing market research is something that makes you a better business person. In business, it's all a part of being in the know of things. When you know then you can go and flow. Don't ever be afraid of the competition. Iron sharpens Iron. Knowing what's happening. Knowing what's HOT in a market is good.

Find out what's moving. Who's selling product similar to yours. Doing your market research helps you stay competitive. It actually pushes you to be better at what you do. Then you can offer better prices and deals. Position yourself for success and come out on top.

I remember one year I went to visit relatives in New York City. At that time, I experienced something I'd never seen before. I'd gone downtown to do some site seeing and shopping. The streets were crowded. The sidewalks were running over with Vendors and business people selling and competing with their goods. They'd moved all their racks of clothing, household goods, jewelry and electronics out to the sidewalks.

What I Saw: If you saw one watch sitting on a table priced at $100.00 all you had to do was keep walking down the sidewalk and within blocks you'd see the same watch drop in price. Even all the way down to $25.00 bucks. It was crazy.

Anyway, I said that to let you know you need to keep to your uniqueness and what makes you stand out, but also need to be competitive without losing your shirt.

Narrow down your specifics of research. Know what kind of business you are and who your customers will be. Let's look at two of the most popular ways that business is being done in this new millennium. The following two scenarios are business marketing terms you'll need to understand before starting your business. What's going on in the two different markets?

The first one is - B2B

The second one is - B2C

Determine if you want to be in market one as a business person.

B2B

Definition: Business that sells products or provides services to other businesses.

Meaning: While business-to-business activity exists both online and offline, the acronym B2B has primarily been used to describe the online variety.

There has been a significant amount of hype given to the potential size of B2B markets-and how much bigger B2B will be than B2C. Despite the potential size, however, some B2B markets may be overcrowded, as well.

Or will your market be number two - a business owner that sells to the consumer. Those consuming customers will become your bread and butter then, so to speak.

B2C

Definition: Business that sells products or provides services to end-user consumers.

Meaning: While business-to-consumer activity exists both online and offline, the acronym B2C has primarily been used to describe the online variety.

B2C businesses played a large role in the rapid development of the commercial Internet in the 1990s. Large sums of venture capital flowed to consumers in the form of free online services and discounted shopping, spurring adoption of the new medium.

An unfortunate thing:

When the capital markets turned sour, however, the B2C companies were among the first to fall, and they fell fast. Many companies tried to follow the herd of investors by undergoing a B2C to B2B makeover.

For awhile after the .com bubble, B2C was used infrequently except when it was followed by "...is dead." However, some analysts still predicted that consumer businesses would thrive online, just not in the way everyone initially predicted.

So when you figure out which way you want to go with your business weather you want to be a B2B or a B2C, that's half the battle.

4 Simple things to do to start your business Research:

Decisions – decisions: When you start your business you must decide on what type of research has to be done. What's needed – where and when to start even. Remember this is you making it happen. It's up to you to make the decision and follow through. Aren't you the owner, president and CEO of your own business? Then you take the lead. You set the meeting. You bring the enthusiasm. No one else will. Now remember, some things you'll already know, just because you're intelligent enough. But other things you'll have to take some real time to research what it is you're trying to invent, manufacture or sell that will bring you some success.

Understanding the revolution of almighty technology: Know that the NET, (internet) and your PC is your best friend. We move too fast sometimes for the normal things of life, less known having a business to keep up with. But if you're going to run with the big boys, you must do business the big way. And that's by staying connected in every way possible. Not owning the electronic devices essential for your business could mean the difference between winning a bid, making that sale or landing a huge client account. So again, take into consideration how much you can invest here. And appreciate what you're experiencing with all of this hands on knowledge.

Knock- knock! Who's there? It's me…TRAFFIC: After you've acquired the electronic devices you need to get started with your business, next you need to use them to push you forward. So go out there and do the research before you put up your tent per se. Example: what's the best location to set up shop? Where's the traffic going to be? Where's the traffic coming from? This goes for both types of business shops: Home Office PC Kind of business and Brick & Mortar.

Whatever way you chose to do business the key to success is always going to be your traffic. You'll needs lots of it at a steady and repeat stream. Either beating down the doors of your email box, or trampling up to the front door step, going in and out of your brick and mortar shop that's sitting on the corner of prosperity road.

You are what you eat: In doing research, especially INTERNET research be careful of the wolves out there. Learn what to look for in scams and don't sink your money into product information and material that don't work. Use the BBB to look up a business and check out who is who. Unfortunately, we've got a good thing going with all the resourceful knowledge and info we can find out there -but just as equally, there's a lot of junk as well. So be smart.

Learn how to catch red flags and pay attention to them. Google search key words and terms that will take you to the true and right information. Sometimes this comes from trial and error, But most times. There's just as many people who want to see you do well and will help you with good information.

SUCCESS METHOD #11 (Living the Dream)

LIVING THE DREAM = Not the Final Destiny

One thing I've learned so well in all my ventures of where I was going. Enjoy the journey while you're in it. Play, take a rest, have some fun while you're working your business and/or ministry.

So what you've arrived. I'm happy for you and for me. But it's not the final destiny. It's only a moment of rest to enjoy where you've come to. So rest up and rise up. You must never be still or stagnant for too long a period. Since our destinies are many. We'll forever be bettering ourselves.

Now where you are at this moment is a place of praise and thanksgiving. You can see some of the fruit of your labor and that feels good no doubt. But give God some glory and ask HIM for your next level.

Now, before we wrap it up, I want to say thank you for taking this little journey with me. I hope you've been enlightened a little and will continue the mission to finding your dream If you haven't already. And to those who've already made positive commitment to your vision and business goals I applaud you in your future success.

Persistence is a vital key to a bright future. In order to live the dream that God has given you, in business or ministry, you must see yourself doing that. You must aggressively keep after it by making each day better and better and by growing bigger and bigger - whatever that is for you. Weather you choose to do an on-line business or go out and start a franchise, or build your own little boutique shop. You're the one who gets to determine how your dream will look. While God's the one who's determined who you'll be.

Remember He's already said in his written Word...

I know the plans that I have for you, declares the LORD. They are plans for peace and not disaster, plans to give you a future filled with hope. *(Jeremiah 29:11)*

Concerning ministry:

It may be to start a bible college or go feed little orphaned children overseas. It may be to build that church He prompted in your spirit. But remember whatever you do...God is with you as long as you put Him as the first priority in your endeavors. Follow these Eleven SUCCESS METHODS and get some benefit from them.

I know we spoke earlier about just one scripture that Solomon mentioned with our Money, but did you know the bible actually mentions money over 800 times? Well it does. I've already mentioned a few money principles earlier on. But time would not allow me to try and go over the 800 times mentioned of course.

But I do want to give you just a few encouragers that God wants us to have money in this life. The Biblical Business Bones Book is just another way...I can give back to my world by sharing some of my experiences of living for Christ, while putting my hands to various business ventures.

God's promise to me says... He'd bless whatever I put my hands to. Besides, He never intended for our hands to be idle. So I hope I've learned something that will be beneficial to you in your steps toward business.

Now, after the little recap, go ahead and check out the scenarios about God's view and YOU concerning success and money.

So if you lack money it's OK to ask for it! The Lord Jesus said..."we have not because we ask not." You can have a desire to want money - because that is God's desire for you.

Recap

- ❖ WAYS = With All Your Support
  Note:

- ❖ HELP = Here on Earth to Love People
  Note:

- ❖ LOVE = Living Out Vital Efforts
  Note:

- ❖ BEING = Best Ever In Necessary Gestures
  Note:

- ❖ ACCEPTANCE = The Assurance that Gives Life
  Note:

- ❖ HONESTY = Holding onto earnest sincere truths
  Note:

- ❖ QUALIFY = Equipped to Compete
  Note:

- ❖ INVESTMENTS = Seeds
  Note:

- ❖ BALANCE = Brought Forward to End Well
  Note:

- ❖ RESEARCH = Just what it is
  Note:

- ❖ LIVING THE DREAM = Not the Final Destiny

NOTES

In various places throughout the bible we've read things like…

- Work with your own hands so you'll have something to give to those in need
- A man who doesn't work is worse than an infidel
- A man that's lackadaisical will quickly come to poverty and so forth…

In order to live the dream of prosperity and success, it simply means I've followed some type of patterns and principles in my process. Below I've put together a few biblical bones scenarios.

Scenarios # 1 – Owe no man anything but to love him.

A Catfish with Bucks:

In this first scenario story - of the fish, it's about a miracle that took place the minute Peter obeyed the words of Jesus. His actions activated his faith, as he moved out to go do exactly what Jesus had told him. Can you imagine Jesus saying something like that to you relating to your business? It was just that simple. Jesus was just that approachable. He said it so that there would be no accusations against them. And so that no one would have any excuse to reject him and the salvation he preached.

We are to be the same way. If we are to win others to Christ while we're out among our business peers. Make sure people see Christ disguised in you as a business owner, minister and so forth. And when they see excellence, they may just be won to the kingdom of God.

When you think about biblical business bones it means you must trust Christ to help you in your business pursuits. Stick to his word. Do what it says. And you'll succeed. And the enemy can't trip you up when it comes to owing no man anything but to love him.

Check it out. Here it is … Jesus said… "Peter, go down to the river and cast a hook without any bait on it, into the sea. Then wait. Expect a fish, because you're going to catch one. Then when you do, take the money out of its mouth and pay the temple tax."

(Matthew 17:24-27)

What's unique about this story is that Peter had a choice to either obey or not. Since Peter was a professional fisherman he could have spoke up and disputed Jesus by letting him know logic says you can't catch a fish without bait. But Peter only obeyed, Thereby, passing this sort of test by trusting in, and depending on Jesus to supply.

Another unique quality about this story is that only Jesus knew where that particular fish was in the timing of the river. And HE knew exactly how much the tax was that the disciples owed. Down to the exact cents, you can't deny it was a miracle.

Do you believe in miracles? They are something that you and I don't have control over. We can't work a miracle, but we can be a catalyst to one. And we sure can receive them. Only if we believe the words of Christ in the bible book and then do what it says by activating our faith to see our miracle. You need your business to grow and earn money? Then believe and achieve.

Scenarios # 2 – From not enough to more than enough

5,000 hungry men

There's another great fish story I like to read often and it's the one where the little boy was generous enough to give away his lunch for a Jesus purpose. It's called the feeding of the 5,000: a story about how Jesus fed five thousand men plus their families, all from small portions which he multiplied. That's right Jesus took something small and made more. It was two tiny fish and five little loaves of bread.

My words to you are to trust the Lord with your business and ministry and he'll make it more than it is. This business book is a faith based book and stands behind Christian principles. We are not ashamed to say its Christ that allows us to succeed. It's His Holy Spirit that helps us to be more than we ever could alone. So HE gets the glory for our successes in life.

The bible says you will receive from God according to your faith.

(EPHESIANS 3:20 NKJ)… 20 Now to Him who is able to do exceedingly abundantly above all that we ask or think, according to the power that works in us,

This verse says two things. God can do more than it is possible for us to even imagine. Second, what He will do in our lives is dependent on the power at work within us.

What is that power? It is the power of His Word, activated by the Holy Spirit. Amen.

Scenarios # 3 – Flowing Money

Seed time and harvest

Scripture tells us in Genesis 8:22 - that … "As long as the earth exists, planting and harvesting, cold and heat, summer and winter, day and night will never stop."

That means in order to get the money to flowing into your business you must first plant a seed and target it toward that goal and purpose. Don't ever let the idea of not having money stop you from planting a seed. You can always find a seed somewhere. I was taught growing up that if you wanted something bad enough you'd make a way within legitimate reasoning to get it.

Example: let's say you want to start your business now. And you don't have enough money to get going. I ask what do you have around the house that you don't use, want or need anymore. It must be something of value to someone else. It must be in reasonable shape and will benefit someone else. Then take that and place it upon e-bay or on craigslist and sell it for little or nothing. You now have a seed. Don't eat your seed, but instead go plant it. Targeting it toward what you want. See that was easy, (smile).

This biblical principle of seedtime and harvest does work and will always bring positive results when you use it. With this little book of biblical business bones, my great desire is to help you "become your business." But for this to happen, you must get a revelation of God's law of sowing and reaping. When you do, it will change your life and your business forever.

From the beginning in the creation of man God talked about seeds. Genesis 1:26-31 describes God's release of authority into His first two people. He tells them that every living thing had seed in it, and they are to be fruitful and multiply. Seedtime and harvest are about multiplication and authority. By the God-given dominion in your life, you have the power to multiply blessings in the earth.

Listen to these words from Proverbs 11:24-25, "There is one who scatters, yet increases more; and there is one who withholds more than is right, but it leads to poverty. The generous soul will be made rich, and he who waters will also be watered himself."

Multiplication power is in your hands. The seed you hold will grow and increase if it is planted and nurtured. Only what you sow can multiply. If you eat it, it's gone. If you sow it, it will come back many times more. The bible book show us that Father God demonstrated the first example of this principle when HE gave His Son, Jesus, as a seed for the harvest of millions into His Kingdom.

OK entrepreneur – business man / woman. My question is do you want the money to flow and keep on flowing? Like I said earlier… "What's in your hands - don't say nothing - because that's not true. If you have to trade in some pop cans or pop bottles you can find some kind of seed. Now according to your faith so be it unto you.

Scenario #4 – Giving Back

Worthy Soil

At this stage of your business you should have seen some major progress by now. You moneys have started to come in and you're sitting pretty on top of that mound of money that's been flowing in consistently.

NOW WHAT? That's a good question to ask. It's now time to give back to society, community and others. You ask "how do I do that?" Check out the keys below.

- **Firstly Honor God –with Rightful Fruits**

Your seed planted in God's hands is the key to miracles. God has told us not to touch the first fruits. They are holy and sacred and belong to HIM not us. Please take the simply instructions to take the first 10% off the top of all monies you make in your business to give them back to God. They are the tithe. And they are your success to many more doors and windows opening up for you.

In the supporting Scriptures we see the following:

Abraham practiced tithing 400 years before the Law was given - "Melchizedek, king of Salem ... to whom also Abraham gave a tenth part of all..." Hebrews 7:1-1

Jacob also tithed. ".. Of all that you give me I will surely give a tenth to You." Genesis 28:22

The Law ratified the wisdom of tithing. "And all the tithe of the land, whether of the seed of the land or of the fruit of the tree, is the Lord's; so it is holy to the Lord." Leviticus 27:30

And lastly, we see that Jesus confirmed the principle of the tithe. "... You pay tithe of the mint and anise and cummin ... these you ought to have done..." Matthew 23:23

- **Secondly Business– Give something back to your own business or corporation.**

Personal Self– Spend a little on yourself when you can. Not splurging, be modest. Just enough to make sure you're rewarding yourself for all your hard work. This encourages you to go on with what you're doing. This gives you a sense of pride and joy. The bible says you're to enjoy the labor of your hands.

- **Thirdly - Society / Community / Charity**

When it comes to giving back there are tons of ways to do this. I'm not here to tell you which charity or foundation to give to, but my best suggestion is to go on line to find a few of your own choice. Always be quick to show your gratitude and appreciation back to mankind for this shows your love for God's creation. There's so much travesty in the world today. Find your place to strengthen and make whole again by helping out a little.

EXAMPLE:

You may choose to help struggling community charities and the disadvantaged. Find missions and global outreaches to share in giving. A few dollars a week or month sure goes a long way where those in need are concerned. The more you give the more you'll receive as the principle of the Word of God says. It's such a great feeling to do this as well. Giving is a part of you. God put this in us when he created us. So don't ignore the prompting of the spirit when it's time to give back. Time, Talent and Money!

When you do this, once again you'll see how it sets you up for nothing but success. When you look up and see God blessing you with so much, please don't lose your humility and generosity of giving something back.

Now go work your dream and have fun doing it - While waiting to see it come to pass.

CONTACT:

Email us at: icreateinspiration53@gmail.com
See other fiction/non-fiction creative books at:
www.icreateinspiration.yolasite.com